The Heart of Prosperity

Other Books by Catherine Ponder

From the Author of the Best-Selling Classic
THE DYNAMIC LAWS OF PROSPERITY

The
Heart
OF
Prosperity

OVER **100** POWERFUL QUOTES AND
AFFIRMATIONS *that can* IGNITE AMAZING
CHANGES IN YOUR LIFE

CATHERINE
PONDER

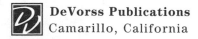

DeVorss Publications
Camarillo, California

The Heart of Prosperity
Copyright © 2015 by Catherine Ponder

ISBN: 978-087516-880-7
Second Printing, 2024

DeVorss & Company, Publisher
PO Box 1389
Camarillo CA 93011-1389
www.devorss.com
Printed in the United States of America

Introduction

✻

"YOU ARE PROSPEROUS to the degree that you are experiencing peace, health, and plenty in your world." Those words are as true today as they were when I first wrote them in 1962 in THE DYNAMIC LAWS OF PROSPERITY. There are no dollar amounts, stock market indexes, real estate values, interest rates, or anything else that may restrict your perception of a prosperous life.

I went on to say, "While prosperous thinking means many things to people, basically it gives you the power to make your dreams come true, whether those dreams are concerned with better health, increased financial success, a happier personal life, more education and travel, or a deeper spiritual life."

My point is that you are the only person who decides what makes you happy, or what prosperity means to you regardless of whether it's 1962 or 2015.

As you start your new journey to prosperity, I feel it's important for you to understand that the process doesn't entail reading a few words and then presto, you're there. It requires work . . . faithful work. Some people struggle, while others seem to breeze their way through and find success patiently waiting for them. It took faithful work for me, and it will take faithful work from you.

If you struggle, don't get discouraged. Whenever I receive a letter from a frustrated student, I point them toward my list of Ten Lucky Steps from page 251 of THE DYNAMIC LAWS OF PROSPERITY to help them regroup and start again.

The Ten Lucky Steps give you a prosperity checklist of what you need to focus on before putting this book to work. I encourage you to take the time to go through each step as a prerequisite to understanding not only the tools you'll need but the role you play in using them.

YOUR TEN LUCKY STEPS

1. Get quiet, meditate, and ask your loving Father (your God, or Divine Intelligence) if there is any reason why you should not become financially independent. This act will remove all uncertainty from your mind, for it is uncertainty that delays your success.

2. Having decided to achieve financial independence and having gotten a sense of peace about the rightness of it for you, make a mental picture of the highest degree of it that you wish to experience. Mentally image the amount of income you wish and how you will live when you are independent. Build as detailed a mental picture of financial independence as possible. The more you think about it, the more detailed your mental picture will become. Think of the kind of home you wish, the type of clothes you wish to wear, the activities you wish to experience, the places you wish to visit.

3. Build the mental picture of what you really want, not what someone else wants you to have, or what you think it is your duty to have – but what you really want. Many people lead miserable lives of failure because they try to please others. Your life is a divine gift for you to live, not for someone else to live for you. Only what you sincerely want can make you happy. Build mental pictures upon that and nothing less.

4. Say little to anyone about your inner plans, because others can always tell you how they think you should live your life, but they can't live it for you successfully. Keep your success plans to yourself. Do not dissipate them, or subject them to cross-current, by giving others a chance to tear them apart.

5. Proceed to take the first steps toward your mental pictures of financial independence. Do whatever little or big things you can to gain the feeling that you are on the way toward it. Set a time limit and plan to achieve certain things within six months, others within a year, and others within two years.

Set a date when you plan to achieve complete financial independence.

6. Do not become anxious, excited, or emotionally upset if affairs do not immediately begin producing the results you desire. Do not try to force or hurry your mental image into fulfillment. Anxious, excited, emotional, hurried, forced states of mind produce violent results that are seldom satisfactory, and they can be most discouraging and destructive.

7. Instead of caring what people say or think, quietly continue to persevere in making your mental image of financial independence come forth, in whatever ways are revealed to you. Remind yourself often that you are working with the rich substance of the universe through prosperous thinking, and that you cannot fail, because the laws of the universe are immutable and cannot fail. Thus, nothing can prevent your success from manifesting, as you keep thinking and working toward it.

8. Realize that your dreams of financial independence
    have already come true on the mental plane by the
    time you desire them or become aware of them.
    Thus, your great good is as much yours before it
    becomes visible as it is afterward, but it is up to
    you to bring it into the visibility. You can do so by
    declaring: Divine substance, give me this now in
    thine own perfect way; or divine substance, now
    meet this demand in thine own perfect way, it is
    mine now and quickly manifests in satisfying ways.
    Never say, "It can never happen," but rather, "This,
    or something better, now manifests."

9. Remind yourself often that if others have attained
    financial independence, so can you. What one has
    done, many can do. What can be done in small degree
    can, with persistence, frequency, and earnestness, be
    done in an unlimited degree. It's up to you.

10. Remind yourself often that every good thing already
    exists in the realm of substance. Through your high
    expectancy, mental images, and prosperous thought
    and action, you become master of the realm of

substance, and can bring forth whatever you wish from it. The history of the world shows that every mental demand of man has been met. Make yours now. Stick to it and you will succeed!

For the first time, here is a collection of more than 100 powerful quotes and affirmations from my book, THE DYNAMIC LAWS OF PROSPERITY, presented in a random format that allows you the opportunity to plant seeds that will spark bold changes in your life. It's as simple as opening a book. Here's what you do:

> Identify and focus on a new direction.
>
> Close your eyes and open to any page.
>
> Open your heart and read the passage slowly.
>
> Begin a new journey to prosperity.

Your perception of prosperity can be determined only by you, so now is not the time to be bashful. The prosperity you choose is the prosperity you will live.

It's time to grow,

CATHERINE PONDER

All Quotes Are from

The
Dynamic Laws
of
Prosperity

The shocking truth

about prosperity is that it is shockingly

right instead of shockingly wrong

for you to be prosperous!

❈

The Shocking Truth about Prosperity
PAGE 11

Prosperity is
your divine heritage.

The Shocking Truth about Prosperity
PAGE 14

Be still, and know that I am God.

Be still, and know that I am God

at work in this situation now.

✻

The Shocking Truth about Prosperity

PAGE 21

God's rich supply
is all around you.

*

The Shocking Truth about Prosperity
PAGE 24

Your attitudes, your mental concepts, beliefs, and outlook are your connecting links with God's rich substance and your access to it.

❋

The Shocking Truth about Prosperity
PAGE 24

I STIR UP THE GIFTS OF GOD

WITHIN ME AND AROUND ME, AND

I AM BLESSED ON EVERY HAND

WITH HAPPINESS, SUCCESS, AND

TRUE ACHIEVEMENT.

The Shocking Truth about Prosperity
PAGE 25

Thoughts of your mind
have made you what you are.
Thoughts of your mind will make
you whatever you become from
this day forward.

※

The Shocking Truth about Prosperity
PAGE 25

Radiate and
you will attract.

✳

The Basic Law of Prosperity

PAGE 32

Each of us constantly uses
the law of radiation and attraction
whether we are aware of it or not.

✺

The Basic Law of Prosperity
PAGE 33

Divine love expressing through
me now draws me all that
is needed to make me happy
and my life complete.

❋

The Basic Law of Prosperity
PAGE 35

EVERYTHING AND EVERYBODY

PROSPERS ME NOW.

The Basic Law of Prosperity
PAGE 37

Choose and radiate mentally;
choose and radiate emotionally;
choose and radiate constantly
and persistently to attract your
own good and good for others.

✻

The Basic Law of Prosperity
PAGE 37

I ATTRACT WHATEVER

I RADIATE.

The Basic Law of Prosperity
PAGE 40

Get rid of what you
don't want to make room
for what you do want.

The Vacuum Law of Prosperity
PAGE 41

If you want greater good
in your life, what are you letting
go of or getting rid of to
make room for it?

*

The Vacuum Law of Prosperity
PAGE 42

Look up
toward prosperity!

✺

The Vacuum Law of Prosperity
PAGE 51

Make room
for your good.

❋

The Vacuum Law of Prosperity
PAGE 54

Strong desire
is success power.

＊

The Creative Law of Prosperity
PAGE 57

I DESIRE THE HIGHEST AND

BEST IN LIFE, AND I NOW DRAW

THE HIGHEST AND BEST TO ME.

The Creative Law of Prosperity
PAGE 58

Prosperity is a planned result.

✳

The Creative Law of Prosperity
PAGE 60

THAT WHICH IS NOT FOR MY HIGHEST
GOOD NOW FADES FROM ME AND I NO
LONGER DESIRE IT. MY GOD-GIVEN
DESIRES ARE RICHLY FULFILLED NOW
IN GOD'S OWN WONDERFUL WAY.

❋

The Creative Law of Prosperity
PAGE 62

Great truths and powerful
secrets often appear simple.

✺

The Creative Law of Prosperity
PAGE 63

As one prosperous thinker has
often said to me, "I find the results
really begin to come forth only
after I start toward them."

❋

The Creative Law of Prosperity
PAGE 73

DIVINE INTELLIGENCE IS IN CHARGE
OF MY LIFE. I AM NOW OPEN,
RECEPTIVE, AND OBEDIENT TO ITS
RICH INSTRUCTION AND GUIDANCE.

The Imaging Law of Prosperity
PAGE 83

You make your
world with words.

The Prosperity Law of Command
PAGE 98

I LOVE THE HIGHEST AND BEST IN
ALL PEOPLE. I NOW DRAW TO MYSELF
THE HIGHEST AND BEST PEOPLE.

✴

The Prosperity Law of Command
PAGE 99

I GIVE THANKS FOR

EVER-INCREASING HEALTH,

YOUTH, AND BEAUTY.

The Prosperity Law of Command
PAGE 101

MY WORDS ARE CHARGED

WITH PROSPERING POWER.

✳

The Prosperity Law of Command
PAGE 102

You can take **your choice**
and follow the high road or
the low road of life.

*

The Prosperity Law of Command
PAGE 105

GOD IS WITH ME TO UPHOLD

AND SUSTAIN ME, AND TO MAKE

ALL THINGS RIGHT.

＊

The Prosperity Law of Command
PAGE 111

The word "prosper" means to thrive or succeed in any given goal or desired objective.

The Prosperity Law of Command
PAGE 112

I AM LETTING DIVINE INTELLIGENCE

THINK THROUGH ME: I KNOW,

I REMEMBER, I UNDERSTAND,

I EXPRESS MYSELF PERFECTLY.

✳

The Prosperity Law of Command
PAGE 113

The Three-Step Formula for Prosperity:

- First, daily write out your notes of desired good.

- Second, mentally image the successful results.

- Third, boldly and deliberately affirm and command those successful results to appear. If you persist daily in following these three simple steps, you will not be able to stop the flood tide of good from overflowing into your life!

❋

The Prosperity Law of Command
PAGE 114

Let your main thought, when thinking of yourself and others, be the thought of riches, prosperity, success, and victorious good.

*

The Prosperity Law of Increase
PAGE 115

Thought of increase turns the tide.

*

The Prosperity Law of Increase
PAGE 116

Never waste your time
giving yourself or others the
thought of decrease.

❋

The Prosperity Law of Increase
PAGE 118

Invoke the law of
increase in simple ways.

✳

The Prosperity Law of Increase
PAGE 120

Give others
thought of increase.

*

The Prosperity Law of Increase
PAGE 121

Give yourself
thought of increase.

✳

The Prosperity Law of Increase
PAGE 122

Hitch your mental image of prosperity to the rich star of success and keep it there.

❋

The Prosperity Law of Increase
PAGE 126

Failure is nothing but success trying
to be born in a **bigger way**.
Most seeming failures are just
installments toward victory!

✺

The Prosperity Law of Increase
PAGE 127

Make the law of increase your new frontier.

*

The Prosperity Law of Increase
PAGE 129

Money is divine,
because money is God's
good in expression.

❋

Prosperous Attitudes toward Money
PAGE 133

There's nothing wrong
with money, or in our
wanting money.

✺

Prosperous Attitudes toward Money
PAGE 135

Since your thoughts make your world, your thoughts about money have to be appreciative in order for money to appreciate you and be attracted to you.

✳

Prosperous Attitudes toward Money
PAGE 137

The golden rule

of prosperous thinking is that you
should not think or say anything
concerning another's financial
affairs that you would want to
experience in your own.

❃

Prosperous Attitudes toward Money
PAGE 139

Even as our national economy
depends on the active circulation
of money, your individual
prosperity depends on the
active circulation
of money.

✺

Prosperous Attitudes toward Money
PAGE 143

I USE THE POSITIVE POWER OF GOD'S

RICH SUBSTANCE IN WISDOM, LOVE, AND

GOOD JUDGMENT IN ALL MY FINANCIAL

AFFAIRS, AND I AM PROSPERED

IN ALL MY WAYS.

✳

Prosperous Attitudes toward Money
PAGE 143

Welcome money
and divine supply
from all directions.

Prosperous Attitudes toward Money
PAGE 144

ALL FINANCIAL DOORS ARE OPEN;

ALL FINANCIAL CHANNELS ARE FREE;

AND ENDLESS BOUNTY NOW

COMES TO ME.

Prosperous Attitudes toward Money
PAGE 144

I GIVE THANKS THAT I AM NOW RICH,

WELL, AND HAPPY AND THAT MY

FINANCIAL AFFAIRS ARE IN DIVINE

ORDER. EVERY DAY IN EVERY WAY

I AM GROWING RICHER AND RICHER.

✳

Prosperous Attitudes toward Money
PAGE 148

Money, money, money,

manifest thyself here and

now in rich abundance.

Prosperous Attitudes toward Money
PAGE 148

Thinking in definite
terms opens the way
for definite results.

✳

Prosperous Attitudes toward Money
PAGE 149

Divine substance is
the one and only reality
in this situation.

✺

Prosperous Attitudes toward Money
PAGE 150

The prosperous,

victorious attitude paves
the way for satisfying,
productive work.

✻

Work – A Mighty Channel for Prosperity
PAGE 154

THE DIVINE PLAN OF MY LIFE NOW
UNFOLDS, STEP BY STEP. I HAPPILY
RECOGNIZE EACH PHASE OF IT, ACCEPT
IT IN MY PRESENT AND FUTURE, AND
LET IT SHOW ME HOW TO MAKE
THE MOST OF MY LIFE.

✻

Work – A Mighty Channel for Prosperity
PAGE 158

Noboby or no set of

circumstances can keep my

God-given good away

from me, and I rejoice in

this knowledge.

*

Work – A Mighty Channel for Prosperity
PAGE 159

Things cannot improve in an
outer way until things change
in an inner way, because
the inner processes of the mind
control the outer experiences
of our lives.

❋

Work – A Mighty Channel for Prosperity
PAGE 161

What is the next step into the
abundance, satisfaction, and freedom
that is mine by divine right?

✹

Work – A Mighty Channel for Prosperity
PAGE 161

NOTHING CAN DEFEAT ME.

I GIVE THANKS FOR THE PERFECT,

IMMEDIATE RIGHT RESULTS.

I REJOICE THAT I AM NOW

SUCCESSFUL IN ALL MY WAYS.

⁕

Work – A Mighty Channel for Prosperity
PAGE 163

I REST EASILY, KNOWING THAT DIVINE
INTELLIGENCE IS RENEWING MY MIND
AND BODY, AND PREPARING ME
FOR AN EVEN MORE SUCCESSFUL
DAY TOMORROW.

❋

Work – A Mighty Channel for Prosperity
PAGE 163

Dare to be a spiritual
architect and to build
pictures of a larger goal.

✳

Work – A Mighty Channel for Prosperity
PAGE 165

I AM NOW SHOWN

NEW WAYS OF LIVING AND

NEW METHODS OF WORK.

❋

Work – A Mighty Channel for Prosperity
PAGE 169

THERE IS NO CRITICISM

IN ME, FOR ME OR AGAINST ME.

Work – A Mighty Channel for Prosperity
PAGE 170

Take a new lease on life
right now, no matter what
your life situation.

Work – A Mighty Channel for Prosperity
PAGE 171

As nearly as you can,

form a mental picture

of what you want your life

to be like.

❋

Work – A Mighty Channel for Prosperity
PAGE 172

After forming
a picture of what you desire,
**begin developing
and living your desire
mentally.** Begin thinking of
the desired results as though they were
already obtained. You thereby take
mental possession of your desired
good and quicken its manifestation.

❋

Work – A Mighty Channel for Prosperity
PAGE 172

Ask Divine Intelligence

to show you the next step toward attaining
your desired picture of good. You will be
shown whether it means going to night
school for more courses of study, making
drastic changes in your work and way
of life, or developing a more constructive
attitude about your present job and its
potential. As you are shown the next
step, boldly follow it in faith, knowing
that it can lead only to richer satisfaction.

❋

Work – A Mighty Channel for Prosperity
PAGE 172

Persist and persevere

in knowing that congenial work can and
shall be yours. Ralph Waldo Emerson said that
everything has a price, and if that price is not
paid, then not that thing but something
else is obtained. So persist in paying the
price in inner and outer ways, and you
shall gain from life what you truly desire.

✳

Work – A Mighty Channel for Prosperity
PAGE 172

Continue giving

your best in your present situation,

even though you may be mentally

living beyond it.

Work – A Mighty Channel for Prosperity
PAGE 172

Tithing brings
definite financial increase.

The Ancient Laws of Prosperity
PAGE 182

Tithing brings
harmonious progress
in relationships.

*

The Ancient Laws of Prosperity
PAGE 185

Tithing brings
peace of mind.

✹

The Ancient Laws of Prosperity
PAGE 187

GOD IS THE SOURCE OF MY SUPPLY, SO

I NOW PUT GOD FIRST FINANCIALLY.

I TITHE MY WAY TO PROSPERITY.

The Ancient Laws of Prosperity
PAGE 198

I LOVE ALL PEOPLE AND

ALL PEOPLE LOVE ME,

WITHOUT ATTACHMENT.

The Prosperity Law of Love and Good Will
PAGE 213

WITH GOD'S HELP, I AM NOW

DELIBERATELY AND JOYOUSLY

RADIATING DIVINE LOVE TO MYSELF,

MY WORLD, AND TO ALL MANKIND.

※

The Prosperity Law of Love and Good Will

PAGE 215

Let divine love
be made alive
in thee now.

The Prosperity Law of Love and Good Will
PAGE 216

I LIVE BY THE LAW OF LOVE,

AND LOVE SHALL BE VICTORIOUS.

❋

The Prosperity Law of Love and Good Will
PAGE 218

Divine love is
in control and all is well.

✺

The Prosperity Law of Love and Good Will
PAGE 221

Divine love
foresees everything,
and richly provides
everything now.

✻

The Prosperity Law of Love and Good Will
PAGE 230

Think big!

Financial Independence Can Be Yours

PAGE 236

I EXPECT LAVISH ABUNDANCE
EVERY DAY IN EVERY WAY IN MY
LIFE AND AFFAIRS. I SPECIFICALLY
EXPECT AND GIVE THANKS FOR
LAVISH ABUNDANCE TODAY!

❋

Financial Independence Can Be Yours
PAGE 244

Build, build, build
your inner mental
pictures of your life.

Financial Independence Can Be Yours
PAGE 250

EVERY DAY IN EVERY WAY

I AM BECOMING FINANCIALLY

INDEPENDENT, WITH THE

HELP OF GOD.

Financial Independence Can Be Yours
PAGE 254

THERE IS NOTHING
FOR ME TO FEAR. GOD'S SPIRIT
OF GOOD IS AT WORK, AND DIVINE
RESULTS ARE COMING FORTH.

Financial Independence Can Be Yours
PAGE 270

DIVINE INTUITION IS NOW WORKING IN
AND THROUGH ME, IN AND THROUGH
ALL CONCERNED, PRODUCING EASILY
AND QUICKLY THE PERFECT OUTCOME,
THE PERFECT RESULT.

Your Genius Powers for Prosperity
PAGE 283

Desire is God tapping at the door of your mind, trying to give you greater good.

✴

Your Genius Powers for Prosperity
PAGE 284

Never underestimate
the power of quietness.

*

Your Genius Powers for Prosperity
PAGE 296

DIVINE PERCEPTION,

REVEAL TO ALL CONCERNED

THE TRUTH ABOUT

THIS SITUATION.

Your Special Powers for Prosperity
PAGE 312

Everything reflects your attitude.

※

Your Special Powers for Prosperity
PAGE 319

NOTHING SUCCEEDS LIKE SUCCESS.
I NOW GO FROM SUCCESS TO GREATER
SUCCESS WITH GOD'S RICH HELP.

❋

The Prosperity Law of Self-Confidence
PAGE 326

I HAVE UNSHAKABLE FAITH IN THE

PERFECT OUTCOME OF EVERY

SITUATION IN MY LIFE, FOR

GOD IS IN ABSOLUTE CONTROL.

✳

The Prosperity Law of Self-Confidence
PAGE 330

INFINITE WISDOM GUIDES ME,

DIVINE LOVE PROSPERS ME, AND

I AM SUCCESSFUL IN

EVERYTHING I UNDERTAKE.

✳

The Prosperity Law of Self-Confidence
PAGE 331

RICH, DIVINE IDEAS NOW COME

TO ME, AND I AM ALL WAYS

ABUNDANTLY GUIDED,

PROSPERED, AND BLESSED.

✺

The Prosperity Law of Charm
PAGE 349

Because we are all bundles of
emotion, a kind word is often all
that is needed to uplift, renew, and
send us forth in a victorious
state of mind.

✳

The Prosperity Law of Charm
PAGE 351

We use the **prosperous power** of Divine Intelligence in wisdom, integrity, and good judgment in all our financial affairs. We give thanks that every financial obligation is paid on time.

❋

What About Indebtedness?
PAGE 365

I HAVE FAITH THAT WITH GOD'S

HELP, ALL OBLIGATIONS ARE

BEING IMMEDIATELY PAID

IN FULL!

❋

What About Indebtedness?
PAGE 368

Indebtedness may appear to be very big in your world, but it need only be a **temporary** situation if you dare to begin believing there is a way out.

*

What About Indebtedness?
PAGE 371

EVERYTHING AND EVERYBODY

PROSPERS ME NOW, AND

I PROSPER EVERYTHING

AND EVERYBODY NOW.

❋

What About Indebtedness?
PAGE 376

I DISSOLVE IN MY OWN MIND AND IN

THE MINDS OF ALL OTHERS ANY IDEA

THAT MY GOD-GIVEN GOOD CAN

BE WITHHELD FROM ME.

✺

What About Indebtedness?
PAGE 377

Dismiss financial mistakes of the past.

✳

What About Indebtedness?
PAGE 379

THE FORGIVING LOVE OF DIVINE INTELLIGENCE HAS SET ME FREE FROM THE PAST AND FROM THE FINANCIAL MISTAKES OF THE PAST. I NOW FACE THE PRESENT AND THE FUTURE WISE, SECURE, AND UNAFRAID.

❋

What About Indebtedness?
PAGE 379

There are **good days** ahead,
there are **rich days** ahead.

＊

What About Indebtedness?
PAGE 382

THE BOUNDLESS, LIMITLESS POWER

THAT CREATED THE UNIVERSE IS NOW

ACCOMPLISHING IN AND THROUGH ME

ALL THAT IS FOR MY HIGHEST GOOD

IN MIND, BODY, AND AFFAIRS.

✻

What About Indebtedness?

PAGE 383

I GIVE THANKS THAT I AM THE
EVER–RENEWING, THE EVER–UNFOLDING
EXPRESSION OF INFINITE LIFE,
HEALTH, AND ENERGY.

✹

Health and Prosperous Thinking
PAGE 410

Nothing in the world
can take the place of
persistence.

✷

The Prosperity Law of Persistence
PAGE 413

I AM NOT ON THE WAY OUT;

I AM ON THE WAY UP!

✻

The Prosperity Law of Persistence
PAGE 414

I AM PART OF ALL THAT

IS GOOD, AND GOOD

SHALL BE VICTORIOUS.

The Prosperity Law of Persistence
PAGE 422

It can and shall happen.

The Prosperity Law of Persistence
PAGE 426

ABOUT THE AUTHOR

CATHERINE PONDER is regarded to be among the most prominent prosperity-success writers/lecturers in the last half of the twentieth century. Author of the long-term best-seller, *The Dynamic Laws of Prosperity* (DeVorss Publications, 9780875165516), she has received many awards and recognitions and is listed in *Who's Who in the World*. She describes her memoir, *A Prosperity Love Story* (9780875167879), as her own personal and professional adventure of "rags to enrichment" – one that now continues into the twenty-first century.